JUICY DRINKS

fresh
FRUIT
and vegetable
juices,
smoothies,
cocktails,
~AND~
MORE

RECIPES valerie aikman-smith
PHOTOGRAPHS robyn lehr

contents

all about juicing

From summer to winter, it's easy to crave juice. Freshly squeezed citrus wakes us up in the morning. Creamy smoothies offer healthy sips on the go. Tall, cool pitchers satisfy on scorching afternoons. And evening cocktails are all the more seductive with fresh fruit or vegetable flavors.

Colorful juices dazzle with splashes of purple, red, pink, orange, yellow, and green. In this book, you'll find a rainbow of fresh colors and flavors. Flip through to a deeply violet pomegranate-blueberry juice, or set your sights on the shocking red of a summer cherry sparkler. Light up martini glasses with delicately pink grapefruit juice, or fill champagne flutes with orange-hued peach nectar laced with sparkling wine. Pour tall glasses full of a sunny pineapple elixir, or enjoy a blend of vegetal green, whipped into an appealingly thick smoothie.

A juicer and a blender are essential tools for many juice-based drinks, extracting pure flavors from fruits and vegetables and whipping them into smooth purées. With the flip of a switch, fresh juices and smoothies are just seconds away. Enjoy a pure, unadorned juice on its own, or look for an exciting twist—many of these recipes feature extra tips to take you from breakfast to cocktail hour in style. There are also a handful of delicious juice-based frozen desserts, from raspberry ice pops to tangerine sorbet to sour-plum granita.

Whether you're juicing for health, blending for fun, or muddling and shaking for a party, this book offers juice-based drinks for every occasion. Bottoms up!

juicing for health

Drinking fresh juice helps boost overall health and well-being in a number of ways:

• Fresh fruit and vegetable juices are rich in nutrients, offering vitamins and minerals, especially vitamin C and potassium.

• Certain fruits such as blueberries and pomegranates also offer disease-fighting antioxidants.

• Smoothies, made by whirling fruits and vegetables in a blender, preserve some of the fiber from the original produce.

• Extracting or blending makes raw fruits and vegetables even easier to digest.

• Drinking raw fruits and vegetables can help you fulfill your recommended daily servings, giving you more in a single glass than you might otherwise consume.

• Sipping juice can help keep you hydrated, providing an energy boost throughout the day.

equipment

An electric juice extractor and a blender, preferably a high-speed model, are essential sidekicks for home juicing. These countertop appliances create fresh, delicious drinks with the flip of a switch. Today's models boast many useful features.

juice extractors

Prized for their separating action, juicers use sharp blades to cut through fruit and extract as much liquid as possible from solids. The action can be circulating, which features a spinning blade; masticating, which evokes a chewing motion; or triturating, which refers to crushing and pressing. Fruits and vegetables—either whole or cut roughly to size—enter through the feed chute. The juice runs out of a spout and collects in a pitcher, while a recepticle collects the dry pulp. This leftover roughage can be used to add fiber to baked goods, or discarded (it's ideal for composting). The powerful processing motion often means a frothy result, varying by the type of produce, but if you let the juice stand for several minutes, most of the froth will soon subside.

Older generations of juicers handled many, but not all, types of produce, from delicate berries to sturdy apples and carrots. Newer models include a second blade attachment that can also tackle fleshy, soft fruits such as peaches and bananas without clogging. Some juicers also have blender features for making smoothies.

Juice extractors readily disassemble for cleaning. The straining basket, blade, pulp recepticle, and pitcher should be removed and cleaned after every use. Many models are dishwasher safe. Before using your juice extractor, be sure to thoroughly read the manufacturer's instructions.

high-speed blenders

Blenders purée fruits and vegetables in their entirety. Unlike juicers, blenders produce little to no waste, and this preserves most of the fiber from the produce as well as offering other increased health benefits. Blending requires a little more prep from the cook. You'll need to remove certain peels and seeds, and roughly chop the flesh to help achieve the most even and smooth results. A blender also needs some liquid to help move the solids down and into the spinning blades.

Blenders vary significantly in quality and price. High-speed, professional-caliber blenders feature an impressive range of speed settings, from pulsing and puréeing ingredients to crushing ice and creating frozen desserts. Start at a slow speed and work your way up, as these motors are powerful. Regular blenders, on the other hand, may not be able to handle ice cubes or firmer solids, so be aware of your machine's capabilities. Like juicers, most units are conveniently dishwasher safe. Be sure to read the manufacturer's instructions before use.

tips for success

Follow these simple guidelines, and juice with confidence:

Know your machine Before you toss in a banana or load up on ice, flip through the user's manual. It can help protect you and your investment.

Chill out If you're planning to serve drinks immediately, start with cold ingredients. Or leave time to pop a pitcher into the fridge for 30 minutes.

Think natural Start with organic whole produce, and trim and scrub it well, so you can enjoy pure juices.

Prep like a pro For blending, pit, peel, seed, and chop, removing anything you wouldn't want to encounter while sipping your drink.

Watch those fingers Use the correct implements to feed pieces into the chute or down the hatch.

Juice in order If you are juicing different fruits, start with those that produce thicker juices, and end with thinner, to help flush out the machine.

Embrace your inner mixologist Transform juices into snazzy cocktails. Page 15 offers inspiration on infusions, ice cubes, garnishes, and more.

the best candidates for juicing

Delicious juice-based drinks begin with ripe, farm-fresh produce. When you head to the market, start thinking about textures and flavors. When possible, shop organic—not a lot goes into juice, so quality ingredients make a difference.

fruits

berries & bite-sized Rinse berries or grapes, grab a handful, and let them tumble down the chute. Hull strawberries, but an extractor can sieve out little seeds such as pomegranates. *Try: blackberry, blueberry, cranberry, raspberry, strawberry, grape, pomegranate*

melons Melons yield large, rewarding quantities of liquid. Select ripe, heavy specimens. Remove rinds and cut into chunks. *Try: cantaloupe, honeydew, watermelon*

stone fruits Peaches and their pitted cousins become thick, sweet nectars. Check settings and use the purée disk if necessary. Choose soft, ripe fruit, and remove the pits. *Try: apricot, cherry, nectarine, peach, plum*

tropical fruits Peel and core pineapples and mangoes. Skin bananas and furry kiwi. Bananas love the blender, but some juicers can't process them; use the purée disk. *Try: banana, coconut, kiwi, mango, pineapple*

tree fruits Crisp apples and pears transform into fresh ciders for fall. Halve or quarter, and remove seeds and stalks. Serve ciders promptly; like their sources, these juices will oxidize quickly. *Try: apple, pear*

citrus An old-fashioned citrus press or reamer will still work, but extracting releases a flood of juice. First, remove the bitter rinds and pith and any large seeds. *Try: grapefruit, lemon, lime, orange, tangerine*

vegetables

stalks & shoots Celery has a mild, likable juice, but bolder flavors are also delicious in moderation. Trim off woody or dry ends, discard the rhubarb leaves, and have fun stuffing whole stalks down the chute. *Try: asparagus, celery, fennel, rhubarb*

leafy greens Dark leafy greens pack mighty vitamins. Combine them with apple juice to mellow the bitter edge. Rinse away any grit, and roll up big leaves for ease. *Try: chard, kale, spinach, wheatgrass*

crucifers Broccoli and cabbage juices have bold flavors, but the health benefits are inarguable. Try them cut with sweet, mellowing flavors such as carrot. Split larger heads for easier handling. *Try: broccoli, Brussels sprouts, cabbage, cauliflower*

vegetable fruits These "vegetables" yield delicious juices, from thin (peppers) to thick (tomatoes). Remove the tough stems, but keep the seeds and ribs to taste. Buttery avocado may require a purée disk; check the settings or opt for the blender. *Try: avocado, bell pepper, chile, cucumber, tomato*

hard roots Carrot juice has a fanatic following, and one sweet, invigorating sip will tell you why. It's not necessary to peel most root vegetables, but trim their greenery and give them a good scrub. Their earthy-sweet flavor often pairs especially well with citrus. *Try: beet, carrot, parsnip, radish*

classic juicy cocktails

Once you start creating delicious juices, it's only natural to reach for a cocktail shaker. The chart below gives the basic ratios for classic juice-based cocktails. Once you develop a taste for these fresh-tasting concoctions, experiment with mixing your own variations.

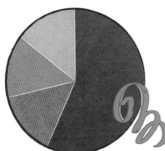  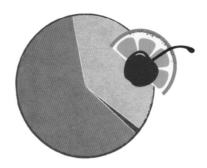

Cosmopolitan
4 parts vodka
1 part triple sec
1 part cranberry juice
1 part lime juice
Lime twist

Margarita
4 parts white tequila
3 parts triple sec
2 parts lime juice
Salt rim

Tequila Sunrise
5 parts orange juice
8 parts white tequila
Splash grenadine
Orange slice
Maraschino cherry

Screwdriver
5 parts orange juice
4 parts vodka
Orange slice

Pimm's Cup
1 part Pimm's No. 1
2 parts lemonade
Cucumber slices
Lemon slices

Piña Colada
1 part light rum
3 parts pineapple juice
1 part coconut cream
Pineapple wedge

Mai Tai
3 parts dark rum
2 parts light rum
2 parts triple sec
1 part apricot brandy
2 parts lime juice
2 parts simple syrup
Dash orgeat syrup

Sangria
6 parts red wine
1 part brandy
1 part triple sec
1 part cranberry juice
1 part orange juice
1 part simple syrup
Orange slices
Lemon slices

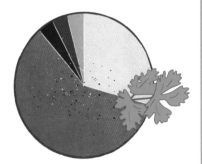

Bloody Mary
2 parts vodka
4 parts tomato juice
Squeeze lime juice
Salt and pepper
Dash Worcestershire
Dash hot sauce
Celery stalk

Greyhound
5 parts vodka
8 parts grapefruit juice
Grapefruit slice

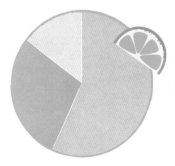

Daiquiri
4 parts light rum
2 parts lime juice
1 part simple syrup
Lime wedge

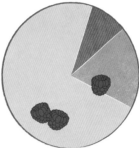

Mimosa
1 part triple sec
2 parts orange juice
8 parts Champagne
Berries

syrups & garnishes

True mixologists stock a selection of exciting sweeteners and inventive garnishes, from herb- and spice-infused simple syrups to whimsical ice cubes. Look to these tips for crafting and serving cocktails with style.

simple syrup

1 cup (8 oz/250 g) sugar
1½ cups (12 fl oz/375 ml) water
Makes 1½ cups (12 fl oz/375 ml)

In a small saucepan over medium heat, combine the sugar and water and bring to a boil. Reduce the heat to medium-low and simmer until the sugar has completely dissolved, about 10 minutes. Set aside to cool (the syrup will be very hot). Use immediately, or transfer to a bottle or an airtight container and chill completely in the refrigerator, up to 14 days.

rosemary simple syrup Prepare the simple syrup as directed, adding 1 small sprig of rosemary to the other ingredients. Cool and chill, removing the sprig whenever the flavor has reached the desired intensity.

more infused syrups Instead of rosemary, try other herbs such as fresh thyme sprigs, mint leaves, basil leaves, or lavender blossoms; spices such as cinnamon sticks, vanilla pods, cardamom pods, allspice berries, whole cloves, or fresh ginger; or tea such as Earl Grey. (Add tea bags to the syrup after simmering, and remove when cool to prevent from oversteeping.)

alternative sweeteners Instead of a sugar-based syrup, you can also try a different sweetener. For a floral flavor, try honey; for a smoky nuance, maple syrup; or for a caramel note, agave nectar.

gorgeous garnishes

Colorful juicy drinks deserve a little extra treatment (especially at cocktail hour).

ice cubes Ice cubes made of juices are beautiful, and come serving time, they'll also add a slow release of flavor. Specialty trays offer shapes from cubes to stars and hearts. Play with colored juices, and tuck in berries, cherries, or edible blossoms.

savory & sweet rims A sugared or salted rim adds flavor and personality. Try mixing in grated zest, minced herbs, or spices such as paprika or cinnamon. Dampen the mouth of the glass with a little water or juice, spread the mixture on a small plate, and upend the glass. Then pour in the cocktail carefully, so you don't wash away your work.

twists The thin, outermost layer of citrus fruit contains a concentrated flavor. Remove with a grater, vegetable peeler, or sharp paring knife, avoiding the bitter white pith underneath. Add the zest last, perching a long piece on a glass rim, twisting and dropping a sliver into a drink, or swirling fine strands into a pitcher.

slices & wedges For quick flair, grab a slice or wedge of what's already on the cutting board. Try cutting the item in a different direction or on a bias to create interesting shapes. Dehydrated fruit can also be very pretty, and many vegetable cocktails love the vinegary zing of a pickle.

BERRY
pomegranate
PLUM
blueberry
POMEGRANATE
GRAPE
BLACKBERRY

PURPLE DRINKS

GRAPE
BLACKBERRY
pomegranate
BLUE
BERRY
grape

Pomegranates and blueberries are full of vitamins and are a good flavor match in a juice. Depending on the tartness, you may need to add a little sweetener to the final result.

pomegranate-blueberry juice

1 cup (6 oz/185 g) pomegranate seeds

2 cups (8 oz/250 g) blueberries

Sugar (optional)

Ice cubes

Sparkling water

Whole blueberries for garnish

FRUITY GIN FIZZ

4 juniper berries

½ cup (4 fl oz/125 ml) gin, preferably Hendrick's

Pinch of sugar

Ice cubes

½ cup (4 fl oz/125 ml) Pomegranate-Blueberry Juice

1 organic egg white (see note)

Tonic water

In an extractor, juice the pomegranate seeds and blueberries. Taste the juice for sweetness and add a little sugar if needed.

Fill tall glasses with ice. Pour in the juice and top with sparkling water. Garnish with blueberries and serve.

MAKES 2 SERVINGS (1 CUP/8 FL OZ/250 ML JUICE BASE)

make it a fruity gin fizz

Muddle the juniper berries, gin, and sugar in a cocktail shaker. Fill the cocktail shaker with ice and pour in the Pomegranate-Blueberry Juice and egg white.

Shake vigorously and strain into glasses filled with ice. Top with tonic water and serve.

Note: This dish contains raw egg. If you have health or safety concerns, omit or replace it with a pasteurized egg product.

MAKES 2 COCKTAILS

Blackberries and apples form a happy partnership in this juice. The berries offer earthy depth, but apples counter with gentle sweetness.

blackberry punch

2 Fuji or Pink Lady apples

5 cups (20 oz/625 g) blackberries

Sugar (optional)

Ice cubes

Halved blackberries for garnish

Thin apple slices for garnish

Club soda

PUNCH WITH A PUNCH

1 cup (8 fl oz/250 ml) vodka

¼ cup (2 fl oz/60 ml) crème de cassis

1 recipe Blackberry Punch

Crushed ice

Quarter and core the apples. In an extractor, juice the blackberries followed by the apples. Taste the juice for sweetness and add a little sugar if needed.

Fill a pitcher with ice and add the halved blackberries and the apple slices. Pour in the blackberry-apple juice, stir, top with club soda, and serve.

MAKES 2–3 SERVINGS (2½ CUPS/20 FL OZ/625 ML JUICE BASE)

make it a punch with a punch

Pour the vodka and the cassis into the pitcher of Blackberry Punch and stir. Fill tall glasses with crushed ice, pour in the punch, and serve.

MAKES 1 PITCHER; 4–6 SERVINGS

Choose firm, sweet plums for best results when juicing. Plum juice quickly turns into a spritzer with Japanese plum and sparkling wines.

plum juice

8 large plums, about 3 lb (1.5 kg) total weight

Agave nectar or honey (optional)

Ice cubes

PLUM SPRITZER

Ice cubes

1 cup (8 fl oz/250 ml) Plum Juice

½ cup (4 fl oz/125 ml) Japanese plum wine, such as Umesha

Plum slices for garnish

1 bottle (750 ml) chilled sparkling white wine

Halve and pit the plums. In an extractor, juice the plums. Set aside for a few minutes to let the foam subside and the juice settle.

Taste the juice for sweetness, and add agave if needed. Fill glasses with ice, pour in the juice, and serve.

MAKES 2 SERVINGS (SCANT 2 CUPS/16 FL OZ/500 ML JUICE BASE)

make it a plum spritzer

Fill a pitcher with ice and pour in the Plum Juice and wine. Add the plum slices, stir, and top with the sparkling white wine. Pour into chilled glasses and serve.

MAKES 1 PITCHER; 6–8 SERVINGS

Dark red Santa Rosa plums are not only juicy and sweet, but give a vibrant color when juiced. Adding fresh ginger gives a pleasant heat that lingers on the tongue.

plum & ginger granita

12 Santa Rosa plums, about 4 ½ lb (2.25 kg) total weight

1 cup (8 fl oz/250 ml) Simple Syrup (page 15)

¼ cup (1 ¼ oz/35 g) roughly chopped fresh ginger

Plum slices for garnish

Halve and pit the plums. Pour the cooled simple syrup into a blender. Add the plums and ginger and process until smooth.

Pour the mixture into a 9-by-13-inch (23-by-33-cm) glass baking dish, cover, and place in the freezer for about 1 hour. Remove from the freezer and, using a fork, rake the mixture into flakes. Return to the freezer and repeat this process every 30 minutes until the mixture looks like shaved ice, about 3 hours total.

Scoop the granita into glasses or bowls, garnish with plum slices, and serve.

Note: The granita can be made up to 1 day ahead of serving. Cover the dish securely with plastic wrap for storing.

MAKES 6 SERVINGS

This is a fun smoothie to make, with a wonderful mix of strawberries, blueberries, and blackberries. Yogurt gives it a smooth, creamy texture.

mixed berry smoothie

2 cups (8 oz/250 g) strawberries

1 cup (4 oz/125 g) *each* blueberries and blackberries

1 cup (8 oz/250 g) plain yogurt

1 cup (8 oz/250 g) ice cubes

Agave nectar or honey

Remove the stems from the strawberries. Put the strawberries, blueberries, blackberries, yogurt, and ice in a blender and process until smooth. Taste the smoothie for sweetness and add a little agave if needed.

Pour the smoothie into chilled glasses and serve.

MAKES 5 SERVINGS (5 CUPS/40 FL OZ/1.25 L)

ICED BERRY MARTINI

½ cup (2 oz/60 g) strawberries

¼ cup (1 oz/30 g) *each* blueberries and blackberries

¾ cup (6 fl oz/180 ml) vodka

Framboise

1 cup (8 oz/250 g) crushed ice

Whole berries for garnish

make it an iced berry martini

Put the strawberries, blueberries, blackberries, vodka, a splash of the Framboise, and the crushed ice in a blender and process until smooth.

Pour the martini into chilled glasses, garnish with whole berries, and serve.

MAKES 3–4 COCKTAILS

BEET
RED
VEGGIE
blood orange
CHERRY
POMEGRANATE
tomato
WATERMELON

RED
DRINKS

blood orange
BEET
VEGGIE
POMEGRANATE
cherry

In cherry season, the markets are spilling over with all varieties and colors. Bing cherries have dark, rich flesh and a deep flavor, which are perfect for juicing.

cherry juice sparkler

3 cups (1 lb/500 g) Bing cherries

Crushed ice

Sparkling water

Whole cherries for garnish

Stem and pit the cherries. In an extractor, juice the cherries.

Fill tall glasses with crushed ice and pour in the juice. Top with sparkling water, garnish with whole cherries, and serve.

MAKES 2 SERVINGS (¾ CUP/6 FL OZ/180 ML JUICE BASE)

make it a cherry champagne cocktail

CHERRY CHAMPAGNE COCKTAIL

Whole cherry for garnish

Kirsch

Cherry juice

Chilled Champagne

Place a whole cherry in the bottom of a chilled flute glass. Pour in a splash of Kirsch followed by the cherry juice to fill one-fourth of the way up. Top with Champagne and serve.

MAKES 1 COCKTAIL

In the depth of winter, freshly squeezed orange juice brightens and refreshes. Blood oranges in particular render a beautiful, jewel-toned juice, a worthy base for dramatic cocktails.

blood orange juice

6 blood oranges

2 teaspoons sugar

1 teaspoon minced rosemary leaves

Ice cubes

Peel, quarter, and seed the blood oranges. In an extractor, juice the oranges.

Mix the sugar and rosemary together on a small plate. Wet the rims of small glasses with a little juice and dip into the sugar mixture. Fill the glasses with ice, pour in the juice, and serve.

MAKES 2 SERVINGS (2 CUPS/16 FL OZ/500 ML JUICE BASE)

BLOOD ORANGE MIMOSA

Blood orange juice

Chilled Champagne

Sugar cube

make it a blood orange mimosa

Pour the blood orange juice one-fourth of the way up a chilled flute glass. Top with Champagne, drop in a sugar cube, and serve.

MAKES 1 COCKTAIL

Pears balance out the sweet-tart of this autumn combination. Fresh cranberries have a short growing season, so frozen berries are a good option; thaw before juicing.

cranberry-pear juice

3 large pears, about 2 lb (1 kg) total weight

One bag (10 oz/315 g/ scant 3 cups) frozen cranberries, thawed

Crushed ice

Halve and core the pears. In an extractor, juice the cranberries and pears. Set aside for a few minutes to let the froth subside and the juice settle.

Fill glasses with crushed ice, pour in the juice, and serve.

MAKES 2 SERVINGS (2 CUPS/16 FL OZ/500 ML JUICE BASE)

CRANBERRY SPARKLER

Whole cranberries for garnish

Cranberry-Pear Juice

Chilled sparkling red wine, such as Lambrusco

Sugar cube

make it a cranberry sparkler

Put a few cranberries in the bottom of a chilled glass and pour the Cranberry-Pear Juice one-fourth of the way up. Top with sparkling wine, drop in a sugar cube, and serve.

MAKES 1 COCKTAIL

You can buy pomegranates already seeded, so this doesn't have to be a labor of love. If you're starting with whole fruit, one large pomegranate yields 2 cups (12 oz/375 g) seeds.

pomegranate juice

4 cups (24 oz/750 g) pomegranate seeds, plus more for garnish

Honey, agave nectar, or sugar (optional)

Ice cubes

Sparkling water

In an extractor, juice the pomegranate seeds. Taste for sweetness and add a little honey if needed.

Fill glasses with ice and pour in the juice. Top with sparkling water, garnish with pomegranate seeds, and serve.

MAKES 2–3 SERVINGS (2¼ CUPS/18 FL OZ/560 ML JUICE BASE)

make it a pomegranate cosmo

POMEGRANATE COSMO

Ice cubes

¼ cup (2 fl oz/60 ml) Pomegranate Juice

¼ cup (2 fl oz/60 ml) citron vodka

¼ cup (2 fl oz/60 ml) Cointreau

Pomegranate seeds for garnish

Fill a cocktail shaker with ice and pour in the Pomegranate Juice, vodka, and Cointreau. Shake vigorously and strain into chilled glasses. Garnish with pomegranate seeds and serve.

MAKES 2 COCKTAILS

make it a
pomegranate cosmo

Root vegetables yield surprisingly mellow, sweet juices. Although these two ingredients may sound like a strange partnership, beets and oranges are a match made in heaven.

beet-orange juice

4 navel oranges

3 red beets

Ice cubes

Peel, quarter, and seed the oranges. Scrub, trim, and quarter the beets. In an extractor, juice the oranges and the beets.

Fill glasses with ice, pour in the juice, and serve.

MAKES 2–3 SERVINGS (2½ CUPS/20 FL OZ/625 ML JUICE BASE)

BEET VODKA TONIC

Ice cubes

Juice of 1 red beet

½ cup (4 fl oz/125 ml) vodka

Tonic water

make it a beet vodka tonic

Fill a cocktail shaker with ice and pour in the beet juice and vodka. Shake vigorously and pour into chilled glasses. Top with tonic water and serve.

MAKES 2 COCKTAILS

There are lots of different varieties of basil, nearly any of which go well with sweet strawberries. This sorbet has a slight savory taste and is an excellent way to end a meal.

strawberry & basil sorbet

3 cups (12 oz/375 g) strawberries

2 cups (16 fl oz/500 ml) Simple Syrup (page 15)

¼ cup (⅓ oz/10 g) packed basil leaves

1 teaspoon balsamic vinegar

Remove the stems from the strawberries. Put the cooled simple syrup, strawberries, basil leaves, and vinegar in a blender and process until smooth.

Pour the strawberry mixture to an ice cream maker and process according to the manufacturer's instructions. Transfer to an airtight container and freeze until firm, about 2 hours.

Note: If you are using a high-speed blender, put the ingredients in the blender, add 3 cups (24 oz/750 g) ice, and process on the frozen-desserts setting.

MAKES 4 SERVINGS (4 CUPS/32 FL OZ/1 L)

Thin-skinned Persian cucumbers don't need peeling or seeding, making them easy to add to vegetable drinks. Add spice with wasabi, horseradish, hot sauce, or minced fresh chiles.

spicy tomato, carrot & celery juice

10 tomatoes

2 *each* celery ribs, Persian cucumbers, and carrots

Juice of 1 lemon

1 teaspoon wasabi paste

1 cup (8 oz/250 g) ice

Celery salt, sea salt, and cracked black pepper

Celery leaves for garnish

Core and quarter the tomatoes. Dice the celery and cucumbers. Peel and dice the carrots. Put the tomatoes, celery, cucumbers, carrots, lemon juice, wasabi paste, and ice in a high-speed blender and process until smooth. Season to taste with celery salt, sea salt, and pepper.

Pour the juice into chilled glasses, garnish with the celery leaves, and serve.

MAKES 4 SERVINGS (4 CUPS/32 FL OZ/1 L JUICE BASE)

make it a bloody mary

BLOODY MARY

1 cup (8 fl oz/250 ml) chilled citron vodka

3 cups (24 fl oz/750 ml) Spicy Tomato, Carrot, and Celery Juice

2 cups (16 fl oz/500 ml) tomato juice

Worcestershire sauce

Celery and cucumber sticks for garnish

Fill a tall pitcher with ice and pour in the vodka, Spicy Tomato, Carrot, and Celery Juice, and tomato juice. Season with a few drops of Worcestershire sauce and salt and pepper to taste. Pour into tall chilled glasses, garnish with celery and cucumber sticks, and serve.

Note: For more heat, stir in 1 teaspoon prepared horseradish sauce with the other seasonings.

MAKES 1 PITCHER; 4–6 SERVINGS

Inspired by a summer soup, this juice features a medley of sweet red bell peppers, tomatoes, and cucumbers. Serve small cups before a dinner, or add vodka and make party shots.

gazpacho cups

4 red bell peppers

2 tomatoes

2 Persian cucumbers

½ red serrano chile

Splash of Spanish sherry vinegar

1 cup (8 fl oz/250 ml) water

½ cup (4 oz/125 g) ice cubes

Salt and pepper

GAZPACHO SHOTS

1 recipe Gazpacho Cups

2 cups (16 fl oz/500 ml) vodka

Smoked paprika for garnish

Halve the bell peppers, remove the seeds and ribs, and roughly chop the peppers. Core and quarter the tomatoes. Slice the cucumbers. Mince the chile.

Put the bell peppers, tomatoes, cucumbers, chile, vinegar, water, and ice in a blender and process until smooth. Season to taste with salt and pepper. Pour into small cups and serve.

MAKES 8 SERVINGS (8 CUPS/64 FL OZ/2 L JUICE BASE)

make it gazpacho shots

Pour the gazpacho into a pitcher and stir in the vodka. Pour into small glasses, sprinkle with the smoked paprika, and serve.

MAKES 8–10 COCKTAILS

make it
gazpacho shots

WATERMELON

rhubarb

strawberry

GRAPE

FRUIT

RHUBARB

BERRY

watermelon

RASPBERRY

PINK
DRINKS

STRAWBERRY

grapefruit

BERRY

RHUBARB

watermelon

RASPBERRY

make it a
greyhound

Lemon thyme adds an herbal scent, giving a nuance that heightens the flavor of fresh-squeezed citrus. You can use any variety of thyme, and there are lots to choose from.

pink grapefruit juice

4 Ruby grapefruits

Honey, agave nectar, or sugar (optional)

Ice cubes

Lemon thyme sprigs for garnish

Peel, quarter, and seed the grapefruits, making sure to remove the bitter white pith. In an extractor, juice the grapefruits. Taste the juice for sweetness and add some honey if needed.

Fill glasses with ice and place a thyme sprig in each. Pour in the juice and serve.

MAKES 2 SERVINGS (2 CUPS/16 FL OZ/500 ML JUICE BASE)

GREYHOUND

Ice cubes

½ cup (4 fl oz/125 ml) Pink Grapefruit Juice

¼ cup (2 fl oz/60 ml) vodka

Splash of Triple Sec

½ teaspoon lemon thyme leaves

Lemon thyme sprig for garnish

make it a greyhound

Fill a cocktail shaker with ice and pour in the Pink Grapefruit Juice, vodka, and Triple Sec. Add the thyme leaves and shake vigorously. Strain into a chilled glass, garnish with a lemon thyme sprig, and serve.

MAKES 1 COCKTAIL

This is a quick, easy, delicious, and thirst-quenching drink to make for a crowd. If you like, serve it in a large pitcher filled with ice, sliced strawberries, and mint leaves.

minty pink lemonade

3 cups (12 oz/375 g) strawberries

1 lemon

½ cup (4 fl oz/125 ml) Simple Syrup (page 15), plus more if needed

1 cup (8 fl oz/250 ml) water

2 drops rosewater (optional)

Ice cubes

Mint sprigs and strawberries for garnish

Sparkling water

Remove the stems from the strawberries. Peel, quarter, and seed the lemon. Place the strawberries, lemon, cooled simple syrup, water, and rosewater, if using, in a blender and process until smooth. Taste the juice for sweetness and add more simple syrup if needed.

Strain the juice through a fine-mesh sieve and set aside.

Fill a large pitcher with ice, mint leaves, and strawberry slices. Pour in the strawberry-lemon juice. Top with sparkling water. Place in the refrigerator until well chilled, about 30 minutes.

Pour the lemonade into chilled glasses and serve.

MAKES 4 SERVINGS (4 CUPS/32 FL OZ/1 L JUICE BASE)

MINTY PINK JULEP

½ cup (½ oz/15 g) torn mint leaves

1 cup (8 fl oz/250 ml) Minty Pink Lemonade

Crushed ice

1 cup (8 fl oz/250 ml) bourbon

make it a minty pink julep

In chilled julep cups or tall glasses, muddle the mint leaves with the Minty Pink Lemonade. Fill with crushed ice and pour in the bourbon. Garnish with mint sprigs and serve.

MAKES 4 COCKTAILS

Perfect for a hot summer day, keep a pitcher of this Latin-style light fruit drink in the refrigerator for sipping all day long. Choose a seedless watermelon that's heavy for its size.

watermelon-lime agua fresca

1 seedless watermelon

2 limes

2 teaspoons honey

¼ cup (2 fl oz/60 ml) water

Crushed ice

Club soda

Lime and watermelon slices for garnish

Peel and chop the watermelon into small chunks (you should have about 6 cups/2 lb/1 kg). Finely grate the lime zest and set aside. Peel, quarter, and seed the limes. Put the watermelon chunks, lime quarters, honey, and water in a blender and process until smooth.

Fill a large pitcher with crushed ice. Pour in the watermelon-lime juice and top with club soda. Stir in the lime zest, garnish with the lime and watermelon slices, and serve.

MAKES 4 SERVINGS (4 CUPS/32 FL OZ/1 L JUICE BASE)

WATERMELON MOJITO

½ cup (¾ oz/20 g) tightly packed mint leaves

1 lime, cut into wedges

Ice cubes

1 cup (8 fl oz/250 ml) white rum

2 cups (16 fl oz/500 ml) watermelon-lime juice

Club soda

make it a watermelon mojito

In a pitcher, muddle the mint and lime wedges with the back of a wooden spoon. Fill the pitcher with ice.

Pour in the rum and watermelon-lime juice, stir, and top with club soda. Pour into chilled glasses and serve.

MAKES 1 PITCHER; 4 SERVINGS

Rhubarb is bitter when raw, but simmered in a simple syrup, it blends into a delicious drink. Vanilla and ginger spice up this seductive cooler.

rhubarb-ginger cooler

5 rhubarb ribs
(about 10 oz/315 g)

½ cup (4 oz/125 g) sugar

½ vanilla bean pod

2 cups (16 fl oz/500 ml)
water

¼ cup (1¼ oz/35 g)
chopped fresh ginger

Ice cubes

Chilled ginger ale

In a saucepan over medium-high heat, combine the rhubarb, sugar, vanilla pod, and water. Cover and bring to a boil, then reduce the heat to medium-low and simmer for 10 minutes. Remove from the heat and let cool. Remove and discard the vanilla pod.

Pour the cooled rhubarb mixture and the ginger into a blender and process until smooth. Strain the purée through a fine-mesh sieve and set aside.

Fill glasses with ice and pour in the rhubarb-ginger purée. Top with ginger ale and serve.

MAKES 4 SERVINGS (4 CUPS/32 FL OZ/1 L PURÉE)

RHUBARB MARTINI

Crushed ice

½ cup (4 fl oz/125 ml) gin,
preferably Hendrick's

Splash of dry vermouth,
such as Noilly Prat

1 cup (8 fl oz/250 ml)
rhubarb-ginger purée

Candied ginger
for garnish

make it a rhubarb martini

Fill a cocktail shaker with crushed ice and pour in the gin, vermouth, and rhubarb-ginger purée. Shake vigorously and strain the martini into chilled glasses. Garnish with candied ginger and serve.

MAKES 2 COCKTAILS

This is a rich and tasty shake that children love. Freeze it in ice pop molds, and you will have a snack ready at a moment's notice. Either way, it's a pretty blend for parties.

raspberry & almond milk shake

4 cups (1 lb/500 g) raspberries

1 cup (5 oz/155 g) chopped raw almonds

2 cups (16 fl oz/500 ml) almond milk

½ teaspoon vanilla extract

1½ tablespoons honey

1 pint (8 oz/250 g) raspberry ice cream

Whole raspberries for garnish

RASPBERRY ICE POPS

Whole raspberries

1 recipe raspberry-almond milk (before adding ice cream)

Put the raspberries, almonds, almond milk, vanilla extract, and honey in a blender and process until smooth.

Put small scoops of raspberry ice cream into tall glasses. Pour in the raspberry-almond milk, sprinkle a few raspberries on top, and serve.

MAKES 5 SERVINGS (5 CUPS/40 FL OZ/1.25 L MILK)

make it raspberry ice pops

Sprinkle a few whole raspberries in the bottom of ice pop molds and fill each with the raspberry-almond milk. Freeze the ice pops until solid, at least 4 hours (insert sticks when the pops are partially frozen, after about 1 hour). The pops will keep for up to 4 days.

MAKES ABOUT 12 ICE POPS

Summer means strawberries, and lots of them. Make icy frappés for daytime, and then turn them into daiquiris at sundown. Edible flowers are a charming garnish.

strawberry frappé

3 cups (12 oz/375 g) strawberries

1 cup (4 oz/125 g) raspberries

¼ cup (3 oz/90 g) honey

2 cups (16 oz/500 g) ice cubes

½ cup (4 fl oz/125 ml) water

Rose geranium flowers for garnish

STRAWBERRY DAIQUIRI

½ cup (4 fl oz/125 ml) white rum

1 tablespoon strawberry liqueur, such as Fragoli

1 cup (8 fl oz/250 ml) Strawberry Frappé

½ cup (4 oz/125 g) crushed ice

Rose geranium flowers for garnish

Remove the stems from the strawberries. Put the strawberries, raspberries, honey, ice, and water in a blender and process until smooth.

Pour the frappé into chilled glasses, garnish with geranium flowers, and serve.

MAKES 5–6 SERVINGS (5½ CUPS/44 FL OZ/1.35 L FRAPPÉ)

make it a strawberry daiquiri

Put the rum, strawberry liqueur, Strawberry Frappé, and ice in a blender and process until smooth.

Pour the daiquiri into chilled glasses, garnish with geranium flowers, and serve.

MAKES 2 COCKTAILS

ORANGE DRINKS

Sweet, ripe mangoes and tart limes are a classic combination the world over. Add a touch of yogurt and rum to make a cocktail version of an Indian-style lassi.

mango-lime juice

3 mangoes

1 lime

½ cup (4 fl oz/125 ml) water

Crushed ice

Peel the mangoes, cut into large chunks, and discard the pits. Remove the lime zest in strips and set aside. Peel, quarter, and seed the lime.

Place the mangoes, lime quarters, and water in a blender and process until smooth. Stir in the lime zest.

Fill glasses with crushed ice, pour in the juice, and serve.

MAKES 1–2 SERVINGS (1½ CUPS/12 FL OZ/375 ML JUICE BASE)

make it a tipsy lassi

TIPSY LASSI

1½ cups (12 fl oz/375 ml) Mango-Lime Juice

½ cup (4 fl oz/125 ml) dark Jamaican rum

1 cup (8 oz/250 g) plain Greek yogurt

1 cup (8 oz/250 g) crushed ice

Toasted shredded coconut for garnish

Put the Mango-Lime Juice, rum, yogurt, and ice in a blender and process until smooth.

Pour into chilled glasses, garnish with coconut, and serve.

MAKES 2 COCKTAILS

Quenching aguas frescas are a must for hot days. Delicate orange cantaloupe flesh is the perfect choice, delicious served alongside a casual outdoor lunch or grilled dinner.

cantaloupe agua fresca

1 cantaloupe

1 cup (8 fl oz/250 ml) water

2 teaspoons agave nectar, plus more if needed

Juice of 1 lemon

Ice cubes

Club soda

Shiso leaves or mint leaves for garnish

Seed and peel the cantaloupe and cut into chunks. Put the melon, water, agave, and lemon juice in a blender and process until smooth. Taste the juice for sweetness and add more agave if needed.

Fill a large pitcher with ice and pour in the juice. Top with club soda, garnish with shiso leaves, and serve.

MAKES 6 SERVINGS (6 CUPS/48 FL OZ/1.5 L JUICE BASE)

make it a **melon martini**

Fill a cocktail shaker with crushed ice and pour in the vodka, vermouth, and cantaloupe juice. Shake vigorously, strain into chilled glasses, and serve.

MAKES 2 COCKTAILS

MELON MARTINI

Crushed ice

½ cup (4 fl oz/125 ml) citron vodka

Dash of dry vermouth

¾ cup (6 fl oz/180 ml) cantaloupe juice

This is a smooth blend of colorful tropical fruits, thickened with potassium-rich banana. Use coconut or almond milk in place of water to make it a satisfying meal in itself.

mango-pineapple smoothie

2 cups (12 oz/375 g) fresh or frozen mango chunks

2 cups (12 oz/375 g) fresh or frozen pineapple chunks

1 banana

Juice of 1 lime

½ cup (4 fl oz/125 ml) water

½ cup (4 oz/125 g) ice cubes

If using fresh, peel and cut the mango and pineapple into chunks, discarding the pits and core. Peel the banana and cut into chunks. Put the mango, pineapple, banana, lime juice, water, and ice in a blender and process until smooth.

Pour the smoothie into tall chilled glasses and serve.

MAKES 4 SERVINGS (4½ CUPS/36 FL OZ/1.1 L)

Use yellow or white peaches for this recipe; either makes a thick and sweet nectar. Keep the skins on to add beautiful flecks of dark orange.

peach nectar

6 yellow peaches, about 3 lb (1.5 kg) total weight

1 cup (8 fl oz/250 ml) water, or as needed

Ice cubes

Halve and pit the peaches. Put the peaches and water in a blender and process until smooth. Check the consistency and add more water if needed (the thickness of the nectar will vary according to the ripeness of the fruit).

Fill glasses with ice, pour in the nectar, and serve.

MAKES 6 SERVINGS (6 CUPS/48 FL OZ/1.5 L NECTAR)

PEACH BELLINI

Peach Nectar

Splash of peach schnapps

Chilled prosecco

make it a peach bellini

Pour the Peach Nectar one-fourth of the way up a chilled sparkling wine coupe or tall glass. Add a splash of peach schnapps, then top with prosecco and serve.

MAKES 1 COCKTAIL

You can use any type of orange here, but navels offer sweetness with very few seeds. The creamy cocktail variation invokes a classic ice cream bar.

orange juice

6 navel oranges

Crushed ice

Sparkling water (optional)

Peel, quarter, and seed the oranges. In an extractor, juice the oranges.

Fill tall glasses with crushed ice and pour in the juice. Top with sparkling water, if desired, and serve.

MAKES 2–3 SERVINGS (2½ CUPS/20 FL OZ/625 ML JUICE BASE)

ORANGE-CREAM MARTINI

2 teaspoons sugar

1 teaspoon grated orange zest

Ice cubes

½ cup (4 fl oz/125 ml) gin, such as Hendrick's

¼ cup (2 fl oz/60 ml) Cointreau

1 cup (8 fl oz/250 ml) orange juice

2 tablespoons heavy cream

make it an orange-cream martini

Mix the sugar and orange zest together on a small plate. Wet the rims of small glasses with a little juice and dip into the sugar mixture. Set aside.

Fill a cocktail shaker with ice and pour in the gin, Cointreau, orange juice, and cream. Shake vigorously, strain into the prepared glasses, and serve.

MAKES 4 COCKTAILS

Fragrant tangerines have a deep citrus taste. Use the juice from this recipe as a base and add herbs, spices, or liqueurs to mix it up and turn it into a custom cocktail.

tangerine juice sorbet

4 tangerines

2 tablespoons honey, preferably orange blossom

4 cups (2 lb/1 kg) ice cubes

Finely grate the tangerine zest. Peel, quarter, and seed the tangerines. Place the zest, tangerine quarters, honey, and ice in a blender and process until smooth.

Pour the purée into an ice cream maker and process according to the manufacturer's instructions. Transfer to an airtight container and freeze until firm, about 2 hours.

MAKES 5 SERVINGS (5 CUPS/40 FL OZ/1.25 L)

TANGERINE-VODKA SORBET

1 recipe Tangerine Sorbet

Citron vodka

Dried or fresh orange slices for garnish

make it tangerine-vodka sorbet

Scoop the tangerine sorbet into glasses or bowls and pour a shot of vodka over each. Garnish with orange slices and serve.

MAKES 4–6 SERVINGS

Start the day with this healthful blend, which uses staple ingredients probably already in the crisper. If you like, multiply the recipe and serve it in a pretty pitcher.

orange, carrot & celery juice

4 navel oranges

4 celery ribs

8 carrots

Celery sticks with leaves for garnish

Peel, quarter, and seed the oranges. Trim and scrub the celery ribs and carrots. In an extractor, juice the oranges followed by the celery ribs and carrots.

Pour the juice into chilled glasses, garnish with the celery sticks, and serve.

MAKES 2 SERVINGS (2¼ CUPS/18 FL OZ/560 ML JUICE BASE)

GARDEN-VARIETY COCKTAIL

Ice cubes

¼ cup (2 fl oz/60 ml) citron vodka

½ cup (4 fl oz/125 ml) Orange, Carrot, and Celery Juice

Celery sticks with leaves for garnish

make it a garden-variety cocktail

Fill a cocktail shaker with ice and pour in the vodka and the Orange, Carrot, and Celery Juice. Shake vigorously and strain into chilled glasses. Garnish with celery sticks and serve.

MAKES 2 COCKTAILS

YELLOW DRINKS

make it a
meyer lemon drop

Seek out Meyer lemons in the winter and early spring. Sweet and aromatic, their character shines in fresh and simple drinks and desserts.

meyer lemonade

20 Meyer lemons

Ice cubes

1 cup (8 fl oz/250 ml) Simple Syrup (page 15), plus more if needed

Sparkling water

Lemon verbena sprigs for garnish

Finely grate the zest from 5 of the lemons and set aside. Peel, quarter, and seed all of the lemons. In an extractor, juice the lemons.

Fill a tall pitcher with ice and pour in the juice and the cooled simple syrup. Taste for sweetness and add more simple syrup if needed. Add the lemon zest, stir, and top with sparkling water.

Fill glasses with ice and pour in the lemonade. Garnish with lemon verbena sprigs and serve.

MAKES 5 SERVINGS (5 CUPS/40 FL OZ/1.25 L LEMONADE BASE)

MEYER LEMON DROP

Crushed ice

¼ cup (2 fl oz/60 ml) citron vodka

2 teaspoons Limoncello

¼ cup (2 fl oz/60 ml) Meyer Lemonade

Lemon verbena sprig for garnish

make it a meyer lemon drop

Fill a cocktail shaker with crushed ice and pour in the vodka, Limoncello, and Meyer Lemonade. Shake vigorously and strain the martini into a glass filled with crushed ice. Garnish with a lemon verbena sprig and serve.

MAKES 1 COCKTAIL

69

Fresh rosemary perfumes this creative spin on lemonade. Freeze it in an ice cube tray to make citrus cubes, which are a delicious addition to a pitcher of sparkling water.

rosemary-infused lemonade

15 lemons

Ice cubes

1½ cups (12 fl oz/375 ml) Rosemary Simple Syrup (page 15)

Water

Rosemary sprigs for garnish

Finely grate the zest of 3 of the lemons and set aside. Peel, quarter, and seed all of the lemons. In an extractor, juice the lemon quarters.

Fill a tall pitcher with ice and pour in the lemon juice and cooled simple syrup. Stir in the lemon zest and top with water.

Pour the lemonade into chilled glasses, garnish with rosemary sprigs, and serve.

MAKES 5 SERVINGS (5 CUPS/40 FL OZ/1.25 L LEMONADE BASE)

PIMM'S CUP

1 Persian cucumber

1 lemon

1 cup (8 fl oz/250 ml) Pimm's No. 1

2 cups (16 fl oz/500 ml) Rosemary-Infused Lemonade

Club soda

Roughly torn mint leaves for garnish

make it a pimm's cup

Thinly slice the cucumber and lemon. Pour the Pimm's and the Rosemary-Infused Lemonade into a pitcher. Top with club soda. Add the cucumber and lemon slices and mint leaves and stir.

Fill tall glasses with ice, pour in the Pimm's cup, and serve.

MAKES 1 PITCHER; 4 SERVINGS

make it a
pimm's cup

Beautiful, dark purple lavender flowers add a touch of the French countryside to any dish. Here they are used to infuse pineapple juice.

pineapple-lavender juice

1 pineapple

1 tablespoon fresh pesticide-free lavender blossoms

Crushed ice

Lavender sprigs for garnish

Peel and core the pineapple and cut it into spears. In an extractor, juice the lavender followed by the pineapple.

Fill glasses with crushed ice and pour in the juice. Garnish with lavender sprigs and serve.

MAKES 2–3 SERVINGS (2¾ CUPS/22 FL OZ/680 ML JUICE BASE)

make it a french martini

FRENCH MARTINI

Ice cubes

¼ cup (2 fl oz/60 ml) gin

1 teaspoon dry vermouth, such as Noilly Prat

⅓ cup (3 fl oz/80 ml) Pineapple-Lavender Juice

Lavender sprig for garnish

Fill a cocktail shaker with ice and pour in the gin, vermouth, and Pineapple-Lavender Juice. Shake vigorously and strain into a chilled glass. Garnish with a lavender sprig and serve.

MAKES 1 COCKTAIL

Fresh pineapples are best in this recipe. Don't fear their prickly skin— it yields quickly and easily to a knife. Add a scoop of coconut ice cream for a decadent dessert drink.

pineapple-coconut milk

1 pineapple

1 can (14 fl oz/430 ml) coconut milk

4 Kaffir lime leaves

Crushed ice

Peel and core the pineapple and cut it into large chunks. (You should have about 3 cups/18 oz/560 g.)

Put the pineapple chunks, coconut milk, and Kaffir lime leaves in a blender and process until smooth.

Fill glasses with crushed ice, pour in the pineapple-coconut milk, and serve.

MAKES 3–4 SERVINGS (3½ CUPS/28 FL OZ/875 ML MILK)

PIÑA COLADA

½ cup (4 fl oz/125 ml) Jamaican rum

¼ cup (2 fl oz/60 ml) Malibu rum

1½ cups (12 fl oz/375 ml) Pineapple-Coconut Milk

1 cup (8 oz/250 g) ice cubes

Pineapple slices for garnish

Shaved coconut for garnish

make it a piña colada

Put the Jamaican rum, Malibu rum, Pineapple-Coconut Milk, and ice in a blender and process until smooth.

Pour the piña colada into glasses. Garnish with pineapple slices and coconut shavings and serve.

MAKES 4 COCKTAILS

Pears deliver a pleasing juice, and this spin on ubiquitous apple cider makes a nice change. The juice turns into a tasty cocktail, too, enticingly scented with exotic, spicy ginger.

pear cider

5 pears, about 3 lb (1.5 kg) total weight

1 small lemon

½ teaspoon allspice

6 whole cloves

Ice cubes

3 cinnamon sticks

Peel, quarter, and core the pears. Peel, quarter, and seed the lemon. In an extractor, juice the pears and lemon. Stir in the allspice and cloves.

Fill a pitcher with ice and pour in the juice. Add the cinnamon sticks and refrigerate for 1 hour to allow the flavors to develop.

Pour the cider into glasses and serve.

MAKES 4 SERVINGS (4 CUPS/32 FL OZ/1 L CIDER BASE)

GINGERED PEAR COCKTAIL

Ice cubes

¼ cup (2 fl oz/60 ml) pear liqueur, such as Belle de Brillet

2 tablespoons pear brandy

½ cup (4 fl oz/125 ml) Pear Cider

1 tablespoon chopped candied ginger

Pear slices for garnish

make it a gingered pear cocktail

Fill a cocktail shaker with ice and pour in the pear liqueur, brandy, cider, and candied ginger. Shake vigorously and strain into a chilled glass. Garnish with pear slices and serve.

MAKES 1 COCKTAIL

The best apple varieties for cider are Pink Lady, Fuji, or Braeburn. Stick to sweet red apples for juicing, and reserve tart green Granny Smiths for cooking.

spiced apple cider

8 Fuji apples, about 4½ lb (2.25 kg) total weight

Ice cubes

2 cinnamon sticks

1 teaspoon ground ginger

MULLED APPLE CIDER WITH RUM

1 recipe Spiced Apple Cider

2 teaspoons whole allspice berries

Zest of 1 orange, cut into strips

1½ cups (12 fl oz/375 ml) dark rum

Cinnamon sticks for garnish

Quarter and core the apples. In an extractor, juice the apples. Set aside and let the froth subside and the juice settle.

Fill a pitcher with ice and pour in the juice. Stir in the cinnamon sticks and ground ginger and refrigerate for 1 hour to allow the flavors to develop.

Pour the cider into glasses and serve.

MAKES 4–5 SERVINGS (4½ CUPS/36 FL OZ/1.1 L CIDER BASE)

make it mulled apple cider with rum

In a saucepan over medium-low heat, warm the cider, allspice, orange zest, and rum. Simmer gently until the cider is warmed through, but do not allow to boil. Pour into mugs, garnish with cinnamon sticks, and serve.

MAKES 6 COCKTAILS

make it
**mulled apple cider
with rum**

GREEN DRINKS

make it a
classic margarita

Freshly squeezed limes fill the air with citrus aromas. This limeade is delicious as is, or it can be used as a base for many types of drinks by simply adding other fruits.

sparkling limeade

12 limes

Ice cubes

2 cups (16 fl oz/500 ml) Simple Syrup (page 15)

Lime slices for garnish

8 Kaffir lime leaves

Sparkling water

Finely grate the zest of 4 of the limes and set aside. Peel, quarter, and seed all of the limes. In an extractor, juice the lime quarters.

Fill a pitcher with ice and pour in the juice and cooled simple syrup. Add the reserved zest, lime slices, and Kaffir leaves and stir. Top with sparkling water, pour the juice into chilled glasses, and serve.

MAKES 2 SERVINGS (2 CUPS/16 FL OZ/500 ML LIMEADE BASE)

CLASSIC MARGARITA

Coarse sea salt

Crushed ice

1 cup (8 fl oz/250 ml) limeade

¾ cup (6 fl oz/180 ml) tequila

¼ cup (2 fl oz/60 ml) orange liqueur

Lime wedges for garnish

make it a classic margarita

Spread the coarse salt on a small plate. Wet the rims of cocktail glasses with a little limeade, dip the rims in the salt, and set aside.

Fill a cocktail shaker with crushed ice and pour in the limeade, tequila, and orange liqueur. Shake vigorously and strain into the salted glasses. Garnish with lime wedges and serve.

MAKES 4 COCKTAILS

Hearty, wholesome greens come in a wonderful variety and they are available year-round. Use this recipe as a base and mix it up with different greens and fruits.

green smoothie

1 pear

1 apple

4 oz (125 g) rainbow chard

2 oz (60 g) spinach (about 2 cups)

½ cup (¾ oz/20 g) chopped flat-leaf parsley

½ cup (4 oz/125 g) ice cubes

½ cup (4 fl oz/125 ml) water, or as needed

Halve and core the pear and the apple, and chop into chunks. Remove the stems and large veins from the chard, and coarsely chop. (You should have about 3 cups/3 oz/90 g.)

Put the pear, apple, chard, spinach, parsley, ice, and water in a blender and process until smooth. Check the consistency and add more water to thin if needed.

Pour the smoothie into glasses and serve.

Note: You can refrigerate the smoothie in a glass container overnight. Give it a good shake before drinking.

MAKES 4 SERVINGS (4 CUPS/32 FL OZ/1 L)

Grapes vary in sweetness depending on the variety, so choose your favorite and enjoy them in this fast and fresh drink. Add spearmint leaves to give it a bright burst of flavor.

green grape fizz

1 lb (500 g) green grapes (about 3 cups)

Crushed ice

Club soda

Spearmint leaves for garnish

4-inch (10-cm) lemongrass stalks for garnish

GREEN GRAPE SANGRIA

2 cups (12 oz/375 g) grapes

2 *each* kiwis and Persian cucumbers

Ice cubes

1 bottle (750 ml) chilled dry white wine, such as Rioja

1 cup (8 fl oz/250 ml) green grape juice

½ cup (½ oz/15 g) mint leaves

In an extractor, juice the grapes.

Fill glasses with crushed ice, pour in the juice, and top with club soda. Garnish with spearmint leaves and lemongrass stalks and serve.

MAKES 2 SERVINGS (1 CUP/8 FL OZ/250 ML JUICE BASE)

make it green grape sangria

Halve the grapes. Peel and slice the kiwis. Slice the cucumbers.

Fill a pitcher with ice and pour in the wine and grape juice. Add the grapes, kiwis, cucumbers, and mint leaves and stir. Place in the refrigerator for 30 minutes to chill.

Pour the sangria into large wine glasses and serve.

MAKES 1 PITCHER; 6 SERVINGS

Pale green melon and bright kiwis mix together in a vibrant frappé. The base turns into a creative take on a blended margarita.

honeydew-kiwi frappé

½ honeydew melon

4 kiwis

1 lime

½ tablespoon agave nectar, plus more if needed

4 cups (2 lb/1 kg) ice cubes

Kiwi slices for garnish

Peel and seed the melon and cut it into chunks. (You should have about 3 cups/18 oz/560 g.) Peel and quarter the kiwis. Peel, quarter, and seed the lime.

Put the melon, kiwis, lime, agave, and ice in a blender and process until smooth. Taste for sweetness and add a little more agave if needed.

Pour the frappé into chilled glasses, garnish with kiwi slices, and serve.

MAKES 5–6 SERVINGS (5½ CUPS/44 FL OZ/1.35 L FRAPPÉ)

BLENDED KIWI MARGARITA

Coarse sea salt

1½ cups (12 fl oz/375 ml) tequila

¼ cup (2 fl oz/60 ml) Limoncello

1 recipe Honeydew-Kiwi Frappé

Kiwi slices for garnish

make it a blended kiwi margarita

Spread the sea salt on a small plate. Wet the rims of cocktail glasses, dip the rims in the salt, and set aside.

In a pitcher, combine the tequila, Limoncello, and Honeydew-Kiwi Frappé. Pour the margarita into the salted glasses, garnish with kiwi slices, and serve.

MAKES 1 PITCHER; 6–8 SERVINGS

make it a
cucumber-jalapeño gimlet

You can use English, Persian, or regular cucumbers to make this cool and colorful juice (peel and seed regular cucumbers). As a cocktail, it gets a kick from a jalapeño chile.

chilled cucumber juice

2 English cucumbers, about 1¾ lb (875 g) total weight

Crushed ice

Radishes for garnish

In an extractor, juice the cucumbers.

Fill glasses with crushed ice. Pour in the juice, garnish with radishes, and serve.

MAKES 2–3 SERVINGS (2½ CUPS/20 FL OZ/625 ML JUICE BASE)

CUCUMBER-JALAPEÑO GIMLET

Crushed ice

1 cup (8 fl oz/250 ml) gin, such as Tanqueray

1¼ cups (10 fl oz/310 ml) Chilled Cucumber Juice

⅓ cup (3 fl oz/80 ml) lime juice

1 tablespoon Simple Syrup (page 15)

1 small jalapeño chile

Jalapeño chile slices for garnish

make it a cucumber-jalapeño gimlet

Fill a pitcher with crushed ice and pour in the gin, cucumber juice, lime juice, and cooled simple syrup and stir. Quarter the jalapeño and add it to the pitcher. Pour the gimlet into chilled glasses, garnish with jalapeño slices, and serve.

MAKES 1 PITCHER; 4 SERVINGS

Wheatgrass is sold growing in small plastic containers at the natural foods market. Highly nutritious, the leaves have a strong earthy aroma and taste, so a little goes a long way.

wheatgrass-carrot elixir

1 container of wheatgrass
(about 1 cup/1 oz/30 g
when trimmed)

4 carrots

Cut off the wheatgrass at the roots. In an extractor, juice the wheatgrass and carrots.

Pour the juice into chilled glasses and serve.

MAKES 2 SERVINGS (¾ CUP/6 FL OZ/180 ML JUICE BASE)

Index

KIWI
GRAPE
plum
BEET
mango
PEAR
chile
LIME
KALE
peach
CHARD
cucumber
FENNEL
TOMATO
POMEGRANATE
cranberry
RHUBARB
honeydew
CARROT
BLACKBERRY
CHE
tang
ban
BELL
ORA
len
CANTALOU
RASPBER
waterme
PINEAPP
WHEATGR
strawbe